It's Dawn

It's Dawn

Jovina Vaswani

Illustrated by
NANDAN PRINCE

ISBN 979-8-218-29216-4

Illustrated by Nandan Prince
Designed & Edited by Tell Tell Poetry

Printed in the United States of America

First Printing, 2023

For my parents, who raised us to believe that we can be anything.

For my brother, who chose to be nice and kind.

Notes from the Author

This was a year of brave beginnings.

I opened up to my therapist about every difficult detail that required processing. This year, I asked for help because I needed it. I fell deeply in love and hoped against hope that it would work. When it didn't, I learnt to let go with grace, uncurling one finger at a time. I read more books than ever and posted terribly personal poems that I might wince at later. But today, I feel proud of them. This year, I embraced the concept of growth and the woman that I am becoming. I told people they are beautiful and kind. I told people how much I care for them, and I showered them with hugs and kisses. I told people that I miss them, and I showed them the poems they have inspired. I also, very sweetly, told some people to fuck all the way out of my life. This year, I let people know what they mean to me, and I set boundaries. I worked hard and rested harder. This year, I dreamt relentlessly and focused on the variables that I get to control. I made mistakes, allowed myself to grieve over them, and apologized when needed. This year, I learnt to be gentler on people, starting with myself.

This was a year of brave beginnings.

My first poetry collection, *It's Dawn*, is a stream of words my heart whispered when piecing itself back. It is a tale of putting one foot in front of another while clutching hope with both hands and carrying love in my backpack. The journey to light is not easy but these poems have held me. I hope they hold you too.

Much love,
Jovina

It's Dawn

At the Cusp of Dawn

I stand at the ocean's edge and inhale the magic of the breaking dawn. The sun is at its softest, reminding me that you do not have to scream to be seen. The waves push and pull against my knees and I stumble, laughing at my lack of balance. I thank myself for not letting go of hope and for refusing to harden under the weight of undeserved experiences. Hurt took so much of me, making me desperate to create something I could call my own—a thing that is full of love and light. This book is what I came up with. This book is my dawn.

Tell me about your dawn, please?

_____

_____

_____

_____

_____

_____

My beautiful baby bud, I promise you'll bloom.
I am pouring my heart out to nurture you.

It Will Get Better

Here's to hearts—
the ones that are lost
and falling apart.

Here's to souls—
the ones that are hurt
while fighting the cold.

The storms shall end.
The dawn shall break.
Thorns pricked,
but roses await.

I Will Not Settle

Last night, my impulse
pushed me to a flowery path,
but I made an unceremonious retreat.
Today, I am taking shaky, baby
steps on the stony road
that leads to my insane dreams.

Walk With Me, My Friend

The magic in the gaps of your beautiful fingers
urges me to commingle mine.
Our amalgamation will discharge into the starless
skies, and illuminate the cosmos.
Can I please hold your hand?

I Am Not Afraid

The sun was fading into the horizon
spilling sleepy colors across the sky.
A softness signaled the beginning of an end
and I ran to find you.
Meanwhile, the sun said its goodbye
and darkness veiled the entire sky.

It would have been a pleasure to stay there,
to not miss a fleeting escapade that feeds my soul.

I do not intend to lose any more sunsets.
Come and stand beside me if you feel like it.
If you don't, I will still be there,
absorbing a stunning miracle—
something as beautiful as that setting sun.

Some Nights, I Still Miss You

Last night, I missed
you in ink that flowed
on diary pages, smudged
by tears my heart wept,
still broken from the day you left.

Darling, these wounds which closed you to love were for your growth. Stop letting them be a tainted filter through which you cannot see the gorgeous world.

Do Not Rein It In

Some of them will ask you to rein it in,
to dim your light for it's piercing their eyes,
my mother told me as she tucked untamed curls behind my ear.
Don't worry about them. They will learn to look away.
You feel so much and that is your gift.
You will discover the wonderful things you can do with it—
the lives you can save, the art you can make, the dreams you can chase.
Never, ever let anyone take this away.

Pieces

Here is the thing, sweetheart—everybody breaks. Your story relies on what you do with the broken pieces.

I have seen superhumans build them into castles with walls a little higher than life's brutalities.

I have seen angels bring them together to form wings strong enough to cut through the air when it is thick with battle.

I feel bad seeing you break and burn. But somewhere in my heart of hearts, I know you will build something new, and this world will be better for knowing what it is.

I will be better for knowing what it is.

Surrender

I had lost the strength to ask for anything anymore.
I looked away from the shooting star I'd earlier wait for.
Do as you please, I whispered to the universe.

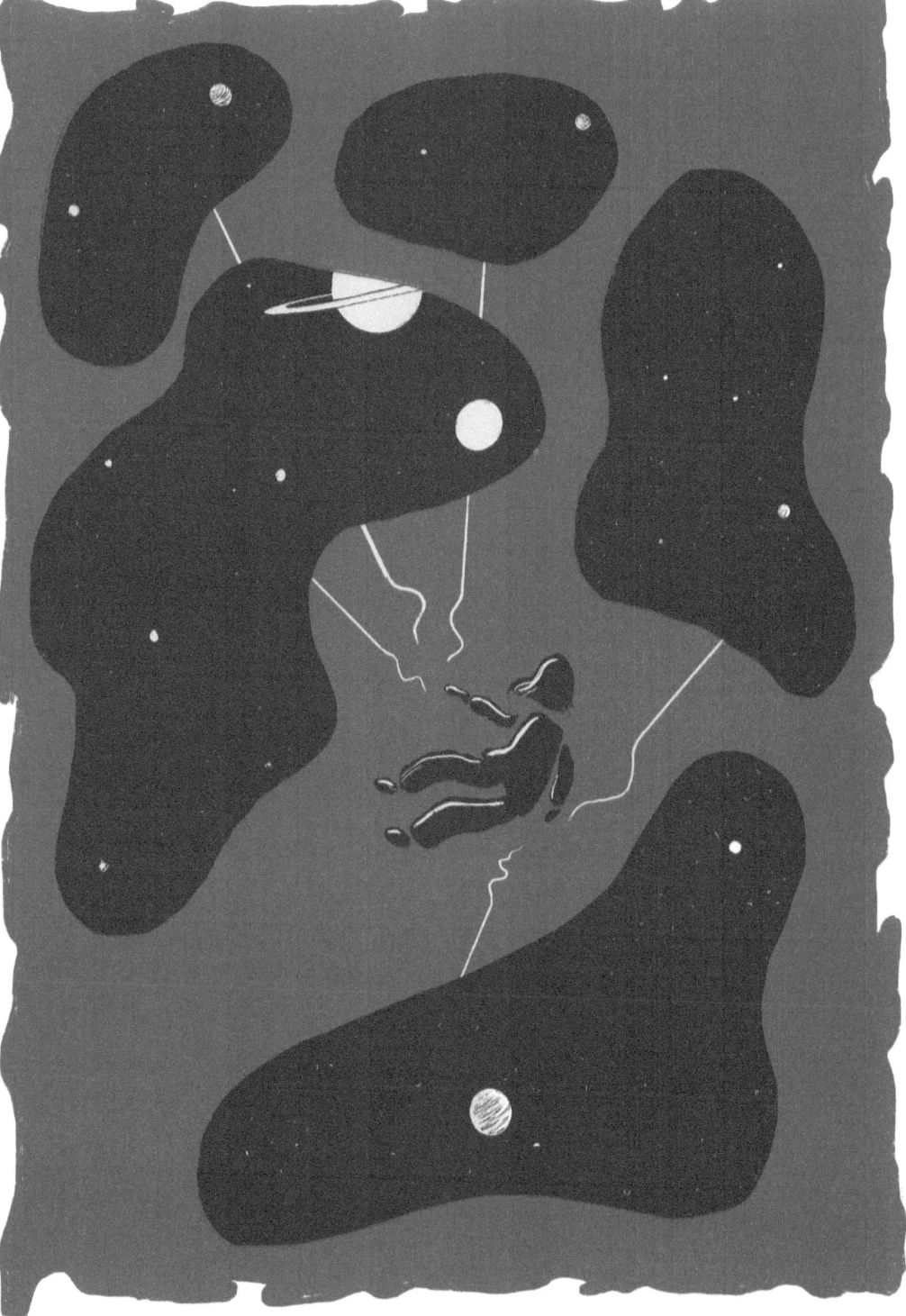

Untethered

You tried confining me to valleys when I had mountains
to climb and oceans to explore.
I did one kind thing for myself—
I let you go.

I Will Not Harden

Unkind words splinter my heart,
but I cradle the fragments with kindness.
I am okay with being hurt,
but not okay with becoming it.

*You are trudging up the slope for the view is gorgeous from the top.
Let it hurt.*

A Fragment of We

Shimmering in the night sky, stars spoke to me,
saying to live by my love for thee.
The winds painted my hair with beautiful dreams
whispering softly in my ears, *never leave.*

With memories and dreams tugged in tight,
there was nothing it seemed which could part us.
Togetherness was all that was there in sight,
but we drifted apart like dandelion bristles.

We drifted apart when we were to stay,
the heart I wore on my sleeve is in a daze.
Darling, you took with you a part of me,
and left me behind, *a fragment of we.*

Redirection

Sometimes, hope hides in the grief of loss.
If you somehow manage to find it,
you will see that it is a one-way ticket
from something you wanted so badly
to something you truly need.

Oh, That Dream

I stopped waiting for you that day, stopped hoping that somewhere down the road, we would end up together. Losing this dream was like draining an ocean, like tossing a chunk of me into the universe. Your voice still moves me in ways words cannot explain, and your smile still increases my heart rate. But I stopped waiting for you that day.

We Will Keep Going

Make your heart an inner compass,
and let your brain adjust the sails.
Your grit will keep you warm,
while the love in you leaves a trail.

July 28th, 2020

I wish there were some recipe, a step-by-step guide I could follow to erase those wounds and welcome new memories to fill a blank canvas. But, instead, the claustrophobic me finds herself inside a tiny attic, dashing from one wall to another, searching for an open door or window, from where I could squeeze out.

It is dark. My scars have the power to obliterate any light that comes their way. Scenarios from the past play in my head like a shuffled playlist and smother me. I do not want to lose myself. I know why I must let go—the question is how?

After weeping as much as I need, I drink a glass of water, grab my favorite book, hug it close, and fall asleep. When I wake up in the morning, I pray to God to keep me steady as I untether myself. In an hour, all the hurt finds its way back to me. I am devastated, but instead of giving up, I tell myself that this is what healing feels like. You give your best every day and it still doesn't feel enough. You are pulled in so many different directions that you cannot move, and when you finally can, it hits that you've got nowhere to go, for home has lost all its meaning by now.

One day, a wonderful person tells me a secret. There is an incredible task God has picked me for. An insane strength is needed to complete it and I will gather that after failing every day in the dark and still doing life. However irrational the little secret sounds, life has not provided an alternative other than catching any tinge of hope that visits me. Hence, before my scars can devour this light, I wrap my fingers around it and place my palm on my heart. As hope seeps into me, I recite poetry into the light.

Flutter your wings hard enough
and the remnants of the past will blow away,
making way for a spectacular flight.

At the Precipice

We were on the brink of something beautiful, and the idea of falling
felt so much like flying. Bravery straightened my wings,
but self-preservation pushed me back.
I know I said I was scared, but in reality,
I was just broken. I worry
I still am.

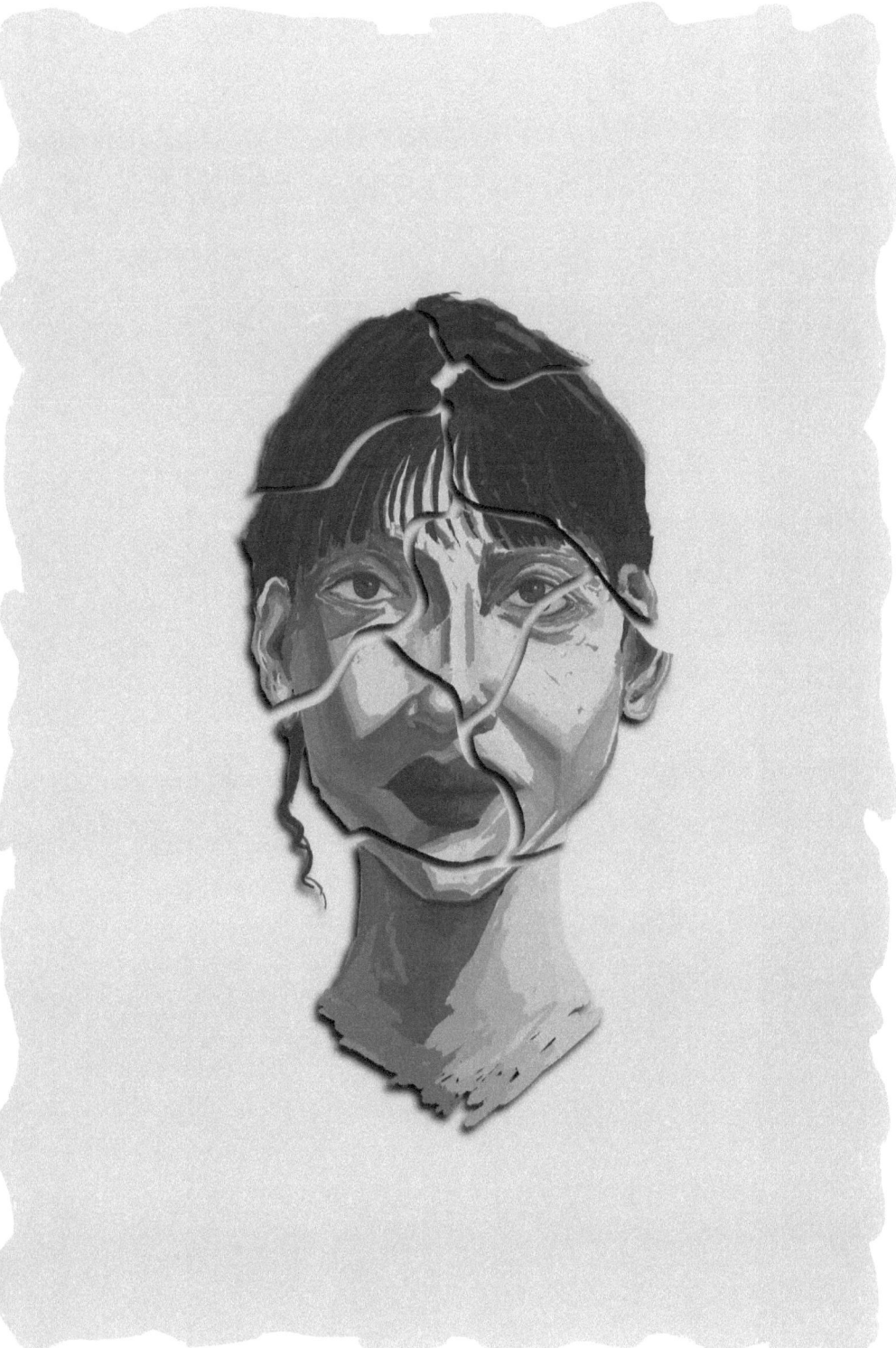

Poetry and I Are Forever

Every once in a while,
my words launch into an orbit around you.
I do not know how to shake from my bones
this innate desire to write about you.
The poems I write do not move you.
Sometimes, you do not even read them,
and so I wonder—
do I really write for you?
Or is it all for myself?

You'll Find Yourself

Oh, but how we lose ourselves
for the things we love!
And then, find ourselves
while healing from their loss.

On Unrequited Love—an (I Thought I Would Never Talk About This) Account

It took a lot that night to stay steady as the sound of your voice echoed in my heart. I noticed your sweet smile. I remember the fluttering.

You held my hand as I spilled secrets on the couch. In the safety of your presence, I found myself falling asleep. I remember the falling.

I told you I love you. What I meant was I love you so much that it overwhelms me. I loved you as if I was never broken or wasn't scared of breaking again. You wrapped me in your kindness, comforted me with everything you had. But I ached. I remember the aching.

I dreamt, hoped, prayed, and wept.
And then, I wrote.
And I am still writing it away.

The world will remember this love,
it will remember the writing.

I Will Be Applauded

I will make something beautiful out of this life.
These broken pieces of mine will collide,
commending my work.
Their clap will sound like thunder,
scaring away everything that ever tried
to take me down.

And when you are tired of navigating the storms,
I hope that your dreams speak to you.

You Are Heard

A prayer is an embodiment of our innocence.
It is an untainted faith that despite everything,
there is somebody, somewhere
who will listen to us.

It Will Get Better

I spoke to life last night.
It feels terrible about the way it has treated you
and promises to be sweeter.
Serendipity will strike you soon
in the most beautiful of ways!
And while handling those lemons,
do not ever forget how much I love you.

Forever a Ballerina

Did I pursue a dream like thunder and still fail? Yes.
Will I stop dreaming? No.
I am a ballerina who would never stop
dancing to the voice of her little heart,
even while the voice is breaking.
Hear me out, darling universe—
I will forever be a ballerina.

Shine Like the Sun

The sun has seen a lot alone, she said as she held me tightly while I wept. *All the injustice and hatred of the world happen under it. It watches in silence—love losing to destiny, hearts breaking of betrayal, and such horrible things happening to such sweet people. Nevertheless, every day, it rises again to illuminate the entire hemisphere.*

This is what you are supposed to do. Show up every day, no matter what life throws at you. You are the light this world so desperately needs.

Shine, little one, shine.

Perspective

It was dark.
But shimmering in all the darkness
were those little *what-ifs*
inspiring me to write a fairy tale.
Suddenly, I knew where to look.

Somewhere in my bones,
I know the waves knocking the air out of me will die,
and I will live.

I Want My Brush Back

Does anyone get to bargain with life? I don't think so. We're presented with a situation, and an option to make the best out of it. Depending on what we decide, we paint our own lives.

I have let things happen to me—let them define what my life would look like. I've been a passive spectator of my life, witnessing it twist into unsettling shapes, entrenching deep marks on my heart and soul. So, whose fault is this? Was the world responsible for building walls around me and protecting my sanity, or was I responsible for standing with my head held high, allowing and rejecting access based on the impact things had on me?

The world has held my brush for too long and I have wept over what it has painted. Now, I want my brush back. I do not have another. This time, I will hold it so tight, the world will give up on trying to snatch it from me. My hands will hurt sometimes, but I will let them. They'll shiver from this big responsibility, and my strokes might not be steady. That's all right. It's my painting, it's my canvas, and it's my paintbrush. It's going to be beautiful. After all, it's the reflection of my soul.

Do Not Suffocate Your Magic

You know you can feel it—
that magic breathing inside you.
Go ahead,
give it to the world.
If you withhold it,
a gorgeous flower
will be nipped in the bud.

Your Star

There's a star that shines only for you.
During moments of darkness,
tilt your head up, and you will find it.
Its light will seep through
the chambers of your heart,
and you will breathe easier.
If you ever need inspiration,
just look up at the sky
and find your star.

Sometimes, Being Held Is an Awakening

Their wings are frozen, and the warmth
of your embrace can work wonders.
Hold them, and as they forget everything for a while,
their wings will be ready for flight.

You're So Brave

What a courageous act it is to open yourself to someone,
to let your rawness unravel as they bask in your light.

We've had our secrets used against us. We've laid our hearts
bare and had them pricked by those who could not handle
such a masterpiece.

But we didn't let pain greyscale rainbows we once dreamt of.
We let our wounds heal.
We let our inner child talk our trust
into loving love, yet again.

Wipe your tears, grab some faith, and jump in to dig your next scoop.
There is nothing, baby, that you cannot do.

Love Makes You Feel Alive

As ably as love can give you wings to soar in delight,
it can also wrap you in blankets of melancholy.
Nevertheless, to be full of love
is to be full of life.

A Moment to Reflect

Slow down a little.
Let it sink in—
the essence of your being.
Embrace who you are,
before you run again.
Just like the sunlight
that slows in the arms
of a water drop. Look
how it bends and breaks
into its true, exquisite colors.

I Love the Way You Shine

Honey, you are the star on the stage of your life,
and you know exactly how to shine.
I am just a spectator cheering with delight,
as I watch my queen slay through the tides.

Uncertainty Scares Me but Does Not Stop Me

I grasped faith with both hands
and jumped in feet-first,
ready to get some things right
and mess up others.
That is now the only way I know of being.

Balance

In the midst of chaos, there should be a bit of peace,
for without it, souls will shatter.
And even peaceful times shouldn't come alone,
for that will numb the souls.

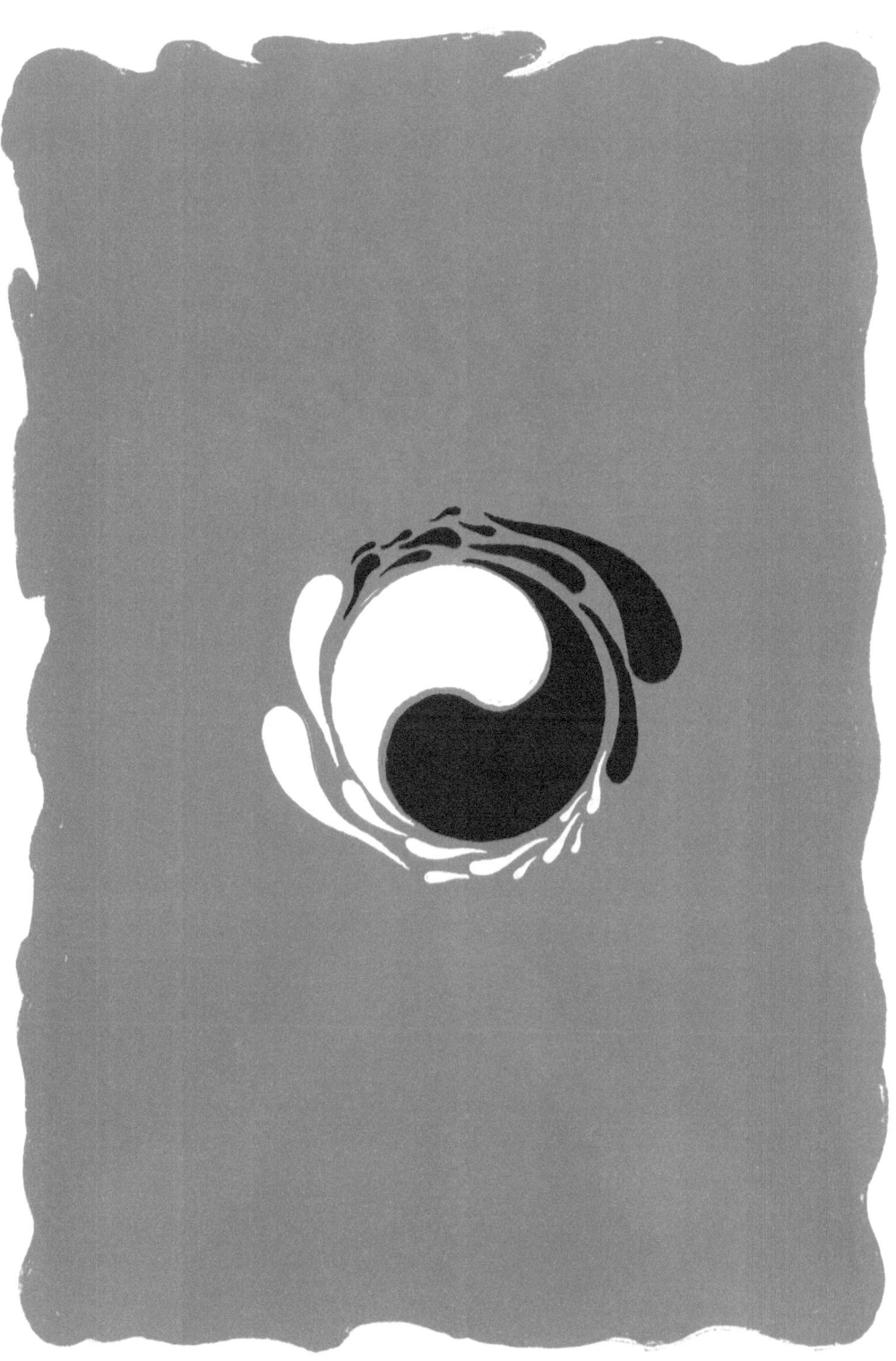

Let love be the driving force for your deeds.
Let it be the lullaby for your insecurities.

I'm Not Done with You (Yet)

Your name sounds like an unanswered
prayer, a hushed longing—there is
brokenness in the way it echoes in me.
But in these cracks, there's unyielding
safety. There's still some hope.

You—a Wholesome Package

Love is what you are made of,
happiness is innate to your soul,
and no matter what it looks like,
your heart is always whole.
Come home to yourself,
look at what is here—
an uncorrupted brilliance
which this world cannot smear!

Your Kindness Can Do Wonders

Be so kind that
their cynicism is strangled,
their happiness disentangled,
their souls are set free.

Be so kind that
they burst into smiles,
and somehow, after a while,
their hearts cease to bleed.

Let Me Help You, Please

When you cried last night,
I saw falling stars in your eyes—
the kind I'd wish on.
During the silence that followed,
I heard my heart whispering truths,
I want to spend lifetimes
cradling your pieces,
straightening your wings,
making sure you can fly.

Am I Worthy?

One night, plagued by self-doubt,
the moon turned to her friend, the lake.
The lake smiled at her friend and
mirrored a radiance so exquisite,
that she happily danced in it.
Tonight, it's my turn to be the lake.
I will reflect the magic you are,
and you will always, always remember it.

There's a reason why hope and home sound so similar.
These are the places where anything is possible.

Keep Fighting

You will begin to love a few people, and they will stand by you in some battles, but not all. Sometimes, some will vanish, or their words and actions will show a lack of trust in your potential. And even if that breaks your heart, do keep fighting. If you wish, keep your door open, but remember, my love, that you're already home.

Feb 13th, 2023
New York City

We slurped strawberry smoothies while walking the Brooklyn Bridge and held hands as we basked in the vibrance of Times Square.

I am falling for this city.

We spent the nights adoring the skyline and slept snuggling with the bliss of found family.

Is it time to leave already? I feel like I just came home

Lift Them Up

Behold the good in them and let them know,
embrace their traits, let them be home,
absorb the beauty of their intrinsic nature,
talk like they are heroes, game-changers.
Emanate the softest, the gentlest vibes,
and they will reveal their hidden light.

Your Light Helps

Your light seeps through my heart and fills it up. It paints strength and bravery onto my soul. It's the sweetest thing I've known. Your light is an intangible magic, a tell-tale sign of warmth, of love, of home.

Things She Says (What They Mean)

The boy is cute but does not have a warm vibe.
(You deserve warmth.)
Call me if you don't feel good.
(I will keep you safe.)
I was just being dramatic—it's what I do.
(It's brave to own the unique snowflakes we are.)
Universe. Take notes.
(I believe the universe looks out for us. You and I will be fine.)
I know you won't judge me. You might yell though.
(We are sisters.)
Missing you right now.
(Even in a room full of people, I will never forget you.)
I was binge-reading your poems.
(I love you and whatever you write too.)

The lightness of your laughter lifts my soul.
You look so much like happiness to me.

I Will Tell You Everything

My heart feels safe with you in it.
Give me a moment love,
and I promise I will tell
you my whole story.
You will not have to read
between the lines.

Admiring You Is Therapeutic

I write happy poems about you
as if my heart is not bruised, my love.
There is something about you
that makes me look past everything,
something that speaks of roses and sunshine and magic.

We've Got This

I believe in you and your magic.
I believe a woman like you can have anything she wants,
must have anything she wants,
will have anything she wants.
Sweetheart, no matter what it looks like,
you've got this,
you've got me,
we've got this.

You Are the One and I Know Why

You make me laugh like a four-year-old, and I wonder about all the laughter that's out there. You're unfailingly kind to me, and I think of all the kindness that graces this world. Your goodness deepens my curiosity for all the good things waiting for me in this lifetime, and gives me hope that I will indeed find them.

My Warrior

I know what all that smile carries,
and it swells my heart with pride—
having vanquished your demons,
it pierces through mine.

When the messes of the world try tearing you apart,
your shattering persistence will shield your heart.

It Will Get Better

I want to go back to my wounded, younger self, stroke
her hair and tell her that we made it.

Even as that little girl, I knew pain like the back of my hand.
However, having become the woman I am now,
I have learnt something about healing too.

It will get better, I whisper to myself as hurt spills down
my cheeks. Because older me would want to come
back to this moment, stroke my hair and say, *We made it*.

Not Every Battle Is for Me

I laid down my sword not because I was tired,
but because retreats from battles
that no longer serve me will
lead me to the ones that do.

Promise Me You Will Stay

Darling, your heart is endless.
Therein dwells the kind of love
that soothes the nerves of the unconsoled,
paints hope on hands wilting in its dearth,
and pours magic upon parched souls.
Stay.
The world needs you.

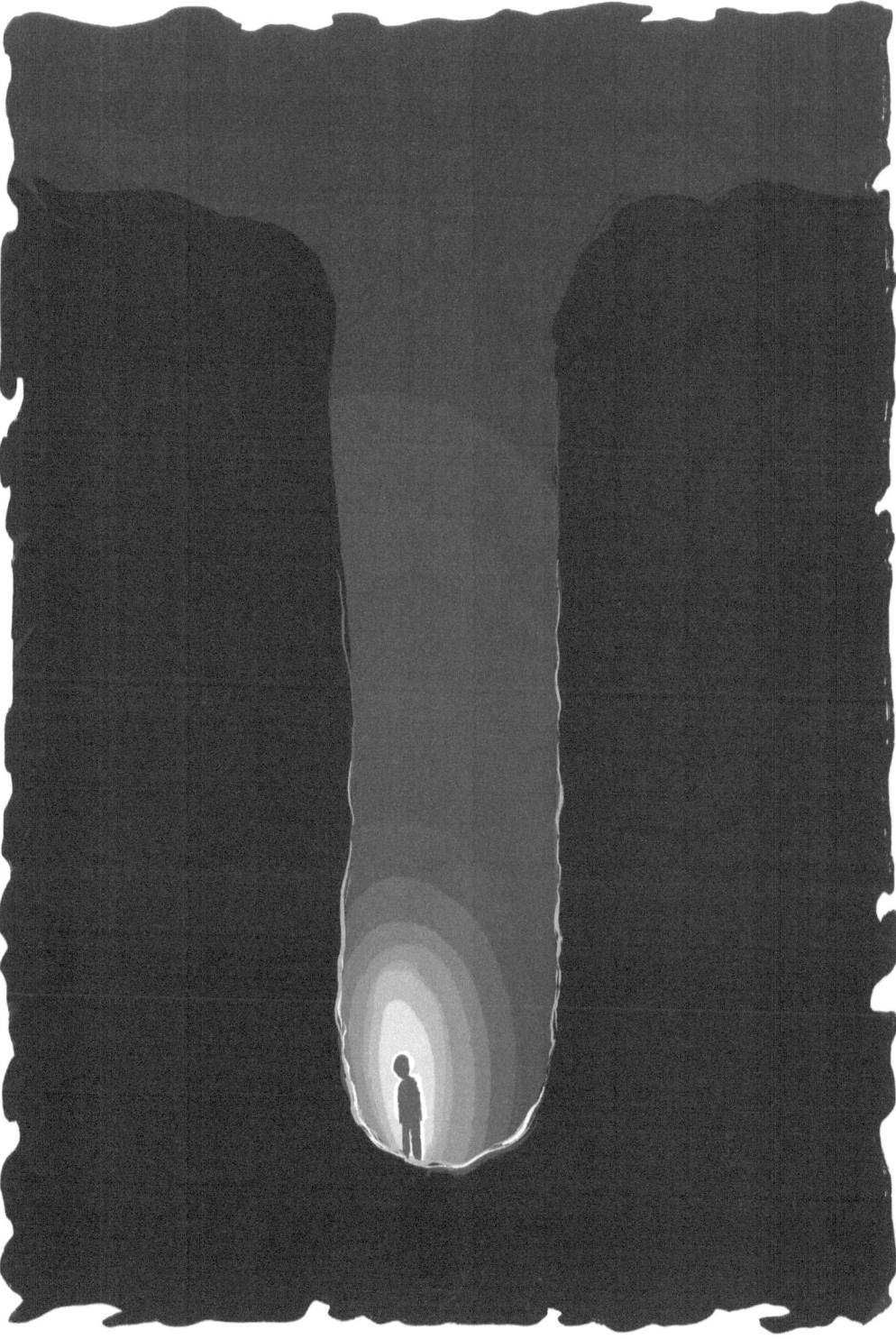

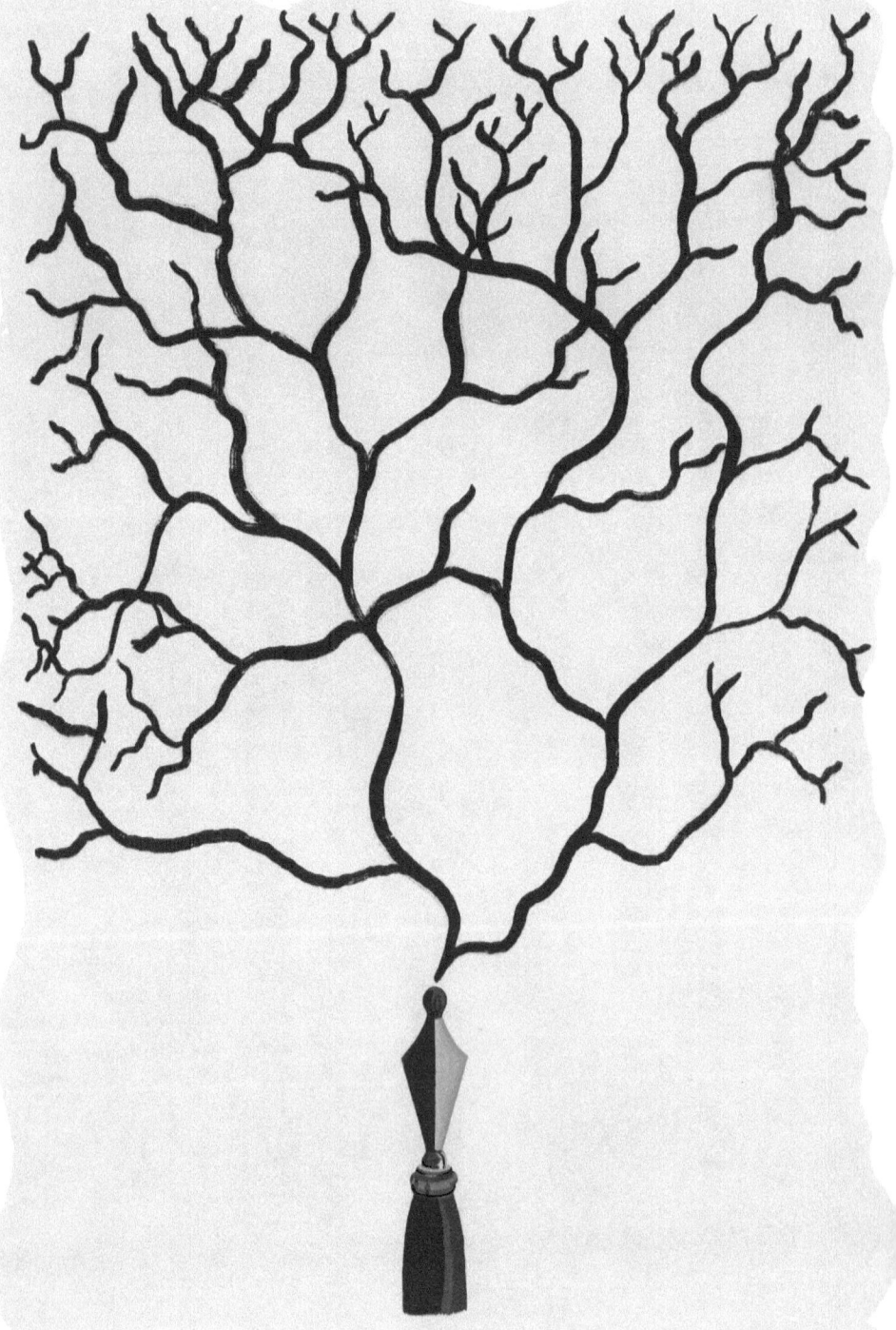

Come What May

Words bled into the cracks of my life,
creating a mosaic of beauty and strength.
As long as the ink flows,
nothing can destroy me.

Life Gave Me Trauma but It Also Gave Me

A mother who prays for me every day. A brother who loves
in silence but not in limits, and a father who'd do anything for me.
A nonbiological sister who sends me her life in voice notes, and
a best friend who lets me sleep beside him when nights cut deep.
A sweet girl who accompanies me to bookstores, and
a friend who loves ice cream as much as I do. Dogs who wag their
tails when I pet them, and their owners who allow me to do so.
A barista who paid for my drink when he saw my puffy eyes, and
a boy who told me I have a good heart even when I was breaking
his. Book endings that make me cry and dedications
that are fucking tender. The gift of expressing vulnerability
and the bravery to confess love. An immense faith
in God and a mother who prays for me every day.

Do not stop now, you little warrior. It's almost dawn.

Contents

There's a reason why hope and home sound so similar

The lightness of your laughter lifts my soul

When the messes of the world try tearing you apart

Do not stop now, you little warrior

About the author

Jovina Vaswani grew up in India with her parents and elder brother. *It's Dawn* is her debut poetry collection, with themes of love, loss, healing, and hope. Writing this book was when she felt the most at home, and she is proud of how fearlessly (and shamelessly) she wove raw emotions into her poems. Her goal is to inspire herself and her readers to reconnect with their true selves and discover the light within. Jovina currently lives in Pittsburgh and is pursuing a PhD in Chemical Engineering. She intends to always be the girl who studies polymer droplets during the day and writes her heart away at night.

www.ingramcontent.com/pod-product-compliance
Lightning Source LLC
Chambersburg PA
20420130626

000006B/2662